Mammals

ANN O. SQUIRE

Children's Press®
An Imprint of Scholastic Inc.
New York   Toronto   London   Auckland   Sydney
Mexico City   New Delhi   Hong Kong
Danbury, Connecticut

Content Consultant
Stephen S. Ditchkoff, PhD
Professor of Wildlife Sciences
Auburn University
Auburn, Alabama

Library of Congress Cataloging-in-Publication Data
Squire, Ann O.
Mammals / Ann O. Squire.
pages cm — (A true book)
Includes bibliographical references and index.
Audience: Ages 9–12.
Audience: Grades 4 to 6.
ISBN 978-0-531-21754-2 (lib. bdg.) — ISBN 978-0-531-22339-0 (pbk.)
1. Mammals—Juvenile literature. I. Title.
QL706.2.S67 2013
599—dc23   2013000091

All rights reserved. Published in 2014 by Children's Press, an imprint of Scholastic Inc.
Printed in China 62
SCHOLASTIC, CHILDREN'S PRESS, A TRUE BOOK™, and associated logos are trademarks and/or registered trademarks of Scholastic Inc.
1 2 3 4 5 6 7 8 9 10 R 23 22 21 20 19 18 17 16 15 14

Front cover: Orangutan
Back cover: Dolphins

Find the Truth!

Everything you are about to read is true *except* for one of the sentences on this page.

Which one is **TRUE**?

T or F   All mammals eat meat.

T or F   All mammals produce milk for their young.

Find the answers in this book.

Contents

THE **BIG** TRUTH!

The Extinction Crisis

A mother and baby orca

Lions use scent to mark their territories.

CHAPTER 1

What Do These Animals Have in Common?

As night falls in a remote corner of upstate New York, a little brown bat wakes up. He has been asleep all day, hanging upside down from the rafters of an abandoned barn. All around him, other bats are stirring. Suddenly, with a whooshing of wings, the entire colony takes flight. Leaving the barn, they fly swiftly and silently toward a nearby lake.

← Bats are the only mammals that can fly.

7

On the Hunt

Nighttime is hunting time for these bats. They eat the flying insects that come out at dusk. As a bat flies, it produces a stream of high-pitched sounds. When the sound waves hit an object, they bounce back to the bat's sensitive ears. This helps the bat determine the size, shape, and position of insects. In moments, unlucky mosquitoes become part of the bat's dinner.

A bat can pinpoint a single, tasty insect to catch even in a mass of insects.

 Orcas and bats both hunt using sound waves.

Orca Mom and Baby

In the icy waters of Alaska's Glacier Bay, a female orca swims with its newborn calf. The baby is just a few hours old, but it already weighs close to 400 pounds (181.4 kilograms). Because the calf has no teeth yet, its mother's milk is its only food. The calf grows quickly. By the time it is a year old, it will have gained approximately 1,000 pounds (453.6 kg)!

An orca pod usually includes related females and their young.

A Long Childhood

Like human infants, young orcas depend on their
mothers for a long period after birth. A baby orca
can swim, but it relies on its mother to guide and
direct its movements. Young orcas stay close to
their mothers. This helps them use less energy
to swim and provides them with protection from
predators. As the baby grows, it learns to hunt
from its mother and other adult orcas in the pod.

A Strange Swimmer

In a small river in eastern Australia, a duck-billed platypus swims just below the surface. It uses its webbed feet to propel itself through the water. Suddenly, the platypus dives to the bottom and begins to poke around in the mud with its rubbery snout. It is searching for food: worms, small shrimp, or even newly hatched insects. But the platypus closes its eyes, ears, and nose when it dives, so how can it possibly find anything?

Platypuses are found only in Australia.

The platypus hunts with electricity. Specialized cells along the animal's bill detect tiny electrical currents created by the prey's movements. As the platypus collects food, it stores the prey animals in its cheek pouches. It then carries them to the surface to eat. These animals are big eaters. A 5-pound (2.3 kg) platypus needs about 1 pound (0.5 kg) of food a day. It will spend about 12 hours of every day looking for its next meal.

A platypus might catch shrimp, crayfish, or other crustaceans to eat.

What characteristics do you see that humans share with this bat?

Same or Different?

At first glance, these animals seem nothing like one another. The bat travels by flying, the orca by swimming, and the platypus by swimming and walking. The platypus and the bat are covered in fur, and the orca lost the hair it had as a baby. The orca and the bat have excellent hearing, while the platypus hardly uses this sense. Do these animals have anything in common? And do they have anything in common with you?

Dogs and other mammals are some of the most popular pets in the United States.

14

CHAPTER 2

Meet the Mammals

The animals we met in Chapter 1 live in different habitats, behave differently, and look very different from one another. But they have something important in common. They are all mammals. Your pet dog or cat, the squirrels and chipmunks in your backyard, and the tigers and lions at the zoo are all mammals. Human beings are mammals, too. But what exactly is a mammal?

People have kept dogs as pets for more than 12,000 years.

A human baby grows in the mother's womb for about nine months.

Mammals are members of the **class** Mammalia. Scientists sometimes divide mammals into two subgroups. Prototherians, such as platypuses and spiny anteaters, lay eggs. Therians give birth to live young. Most—such as humans, whales, bats, cats, and dogs—give birth to young that are well developed. They are called **placental** mammals. Other therians such as kangaroos and koalas are marsupials. Marsupials give birth to tiny, underdeveloped young, which then grow in the mother's pouch.

What Makes a Mammal a Mammal?

All mammals are **vertebrates**, which means they have a backbone and a bony skeleton. All mammals, even those that live in the water, breathe air. They are also **endothermic**, or warm-blooded. Snakes and lizards have backbones and breathe air, but they're not mammals. Birds have backbones, breathe air, and are warm-blooded, but they're not mammals, either. What are the special characteristics that separate mammals from birds and reptiles?

Belugas and other whales swim up to the water's surface to breathe.

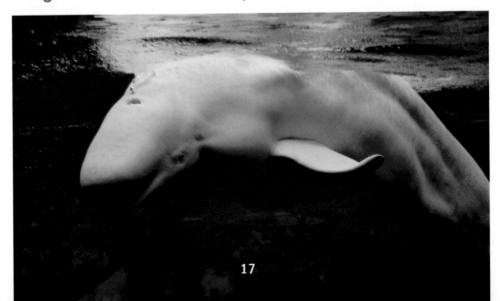

Nursing the Young

All mammals feed their young with milk produced by specialized organs called **mammary glands**. In most mammals, the female develops these glands. Humans and other **primates** have two mammary glands. Animals that give birth to litters, such as cats and dogs, might have eight or more mammary glands. The Dayak fruit bat is the only known mammal in which the male has well-developed mammary glands and nurses the young.

Pigs have 18 mammary glands.

A baby koala, called a joey, spends about a year with its mother.

Learning and Growing

Compared to other animals, mammal parents spend a long time caring for their young. Human children often remain with their parents for almost two decades. In contrast, sea turtles and some other reptiles never meet their parents. Mammals have larger and more complicated brains than reptiles do, and are better able to learn. Spending a long time with parents gives a young mammal time to learn to hunt and protect itself so it can survive.

 The sea otter has the thickest fur of any animal.

Hairy Mammals

All mammals have hair at some point in their lives. The hair on a person's head, the thick fur of a polar bear, and the sharp quills of a porcupine look nothing alike, but they are all hair. Even marine mammals, such as whales and dolphins, have hair. Some **species** are born with fine hair but lose it as they grow. Others have a few hairs around their face or snout.

Jaws . . .

Most nonmammalian vertebrates have jaws made up of several bones. In snakes, this arrangement allows the animal to unhinge its jaw to swallow large prey. Mammals, on the other hand, have just two bones that make up a single jaw. The jaw holds the teeth and attaches directly to the skull. The jaw's structure and the muscles that control it give mammals a powerful bite.

A snake's jaw (left) can open wider than a human's jaw (right). Snakes must be able to swallow prey whole. Humans can cut or tear their food into smaller pieces.

 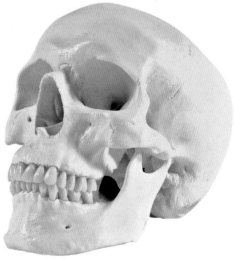

. . . and Teeth

Different mammal species have teeth adapted to their different diets. Meat-eating **carnivores** have sharp, pointed teeth. **Herbivores**, or plant eaters, have flat, grinding teeth. Mammals get just two sets of teeth in their lifetime—baby teeth and adult teeth. In many other vertebrates, teeth are replaced throughout the animal's life.

A jaguar has long, sharp teeth in the front for tearing. Flatter teeth in the back are for chewing.

Jackrabbits use their large ears to listen for predators.

Middle Ear

The final important characteristic that separates mammals from other vertebrates is the number of bones in the middle ear. Other vertebrates have one middle ear bone. Mammals have three: the hammer, the anvil, and the stirrup. These tiny bones transmit vibrations from the eardrum to the inner ear. Because of this arrangement, mammals are generally better at detecting sounds than birds or reptiles are.

Unusual Mammal

An echidna's body is covered in coarse fur and spines. Its slender snout, called a beak, ends with a tiny mouth. Its long, sticky tongue laps up insects and worms. The echidna also has plates instead of teeth and rear feet that point backward!

A mother echidna lays a single egg into a pouch on her belly. After hatching, the baby echidna, or puggle, stays in the mother's pouch, drinking milk that oozes from her skin. When the baby's spines begin to grow, the mother digs a burrow and puts the puggle inside it. She returns every few days to feed the baby until it can survive on its own.

Quick Facts About Some Common Placental Mammals

Group (number of species)	Diet	Distribution	Life Span
Hoofed animals (approximately 165)	Most are herbivores; pigs also eat meat	Found worldwide, except Antarctica	8 to 40 years, depending on species
Carnivorans, such as dogs, cats, bears, and seals (approximately 270)	Most are carnivores; the giant panda is herbivorous	Found worldwide	Most live 10 to 40 years or more; some small species may live less than a year
Primates (approximately 300)	Omnivores, or animals that eat both plants and meat	Nonhuman primates: Africa, Asia, South and Central America. Human primates: worldwide.	Nonhuman primates: approximately 10 to 50 years, depending on species
Rabbits, pikas, and hares (approximately 80)	Herbivores	Found worldwide, except Antarctica	Up to about 12 years, though often less than a year
Moles, hedgehogs, and other insect-eating mammals (approximately 375)	Insectivores, or animals that eat insects	Found worldwide, except Antarctica and Australia	Usually about a year
Whales, dolphins, and porpoises (approximately 90)	Carnivores	Found worldwide	Most live at least 20 years; some may live as long as 200 years
Rodents (approximately 2,500)	Omnivores	Found worldwide, except Antarctica	Most live 5 years or less; a few species may live longer
Bats (approximately 1,200)	Most are insectivores, but some eat primarily fruit	Found worldwide, except Arctic and Antarctic regions	10 to 25 years
Elephants (3)	Herbivores	Africa, India, Southeast Asia	60 to 70 years

The Arctic fox lives in some of Earth's coldest regions.

CHAPTER 3

Habitats and Food

Mammals are found all over the world, from the Arctic tundra to tropical rain forests. One reason mammals can survive in such a variety of climates is that they are warm-blooded. This means they keep their body temperature at a constant level regardless of how cold or hot it is outside. Mammals live in water, on grassy plains, in dense jungles, and in many other habitats. Every species has adaptations to thrive in its particular surroundings.

← The Arctic fox's white fur helps it blend in with its snowy surroundings.

Living in the Water

Harbor seals, like other marine mammals, are perfectly adapted to life at sea. Their smooth, streamlined bodies cut through the water with ease. A thick layer of blubber keeps them warm in the cold ocean. They can dive up to 1,500 feet (457.2 meters) below the surface in search of food and remain submerged, holding their breath, for 40 minutes. When diving, the seal closes its nostrils and ear openings to keep water out.

Harbor seals spend about half of their time in the water.

28

A giraffe eats more than 65 pounds (29.5 kg) of leaves a day.

On the African Plains

Thanks to its long neck, a giraffe can graze on leaves that no other animals can reach. Its thick, leathery lips and long tongue strip leaves from treetop branches. Its splotchy coat helps it hide from predators, and its fringed tail can be used as a flyswatter. The giraffe has excellent vision, so it can spot enemies from far away. If danger threatens, its long legs help it escape at up to 35 miles (56.3 kilometers) per hour.

Cheetahs sprint at up to 71 miles per hour (114.3 kph) to catch speedy prey such as warthogs.

Cheetahs hunt gazelles and other fast-moving animals. The cheetah must be quicker than its prey, and this cat is built to run. Long legs and a flexible spine help the cheetah cover a lot of ground. Ridged pads on the feet and blunt claws provide traction. The small head reduces wind resistance, the flattened tail serves as a rudder, and black teardrop markings below the eyes reduce glare from the sun.

Polar Bear Habitat

Some mammals migrate, or move. Polar bears like to hunt around the edges of Arctic ice sheets, where they catch seals and other marine animals. The ice grows and shrinks with the seasons. Many polar bears migrate south as the ice extends during winter, then north as the weather warms and the ice shrinks. This map shows the normal polar bear habitat and where it can extend during colder months.

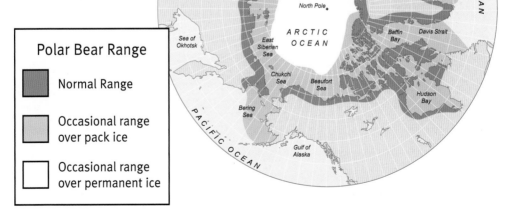

Polar Bear Range

Normal Range

Occasional range over pack ice

Occasional range over permanent ice

North Sea

Barents Sea

Norwegian Sea

Greenland Sea

Denmark Strait

ATLANTIC OCEAN

North Pole

ARCTIC OCEAN

Sea of Okhotsk

East Siberian Sea

Baffin Bay

Davis Strait

Chukchi Sea

Beaufort Sea

Hudson Bay

Bering Sea

PACIFIC OCEAN

Gulf of Alaska

The Extinction Crisis

According to the International Union for Conservation of Nature, half of all mammal species are declining in numbers. One in four species may soon become extinct.

It is not just land mammals that are in danger. Marine mammals such as whales, seals, sea lions, and manatees are threatened by commercial hunting, accidental capture in fishing nets, and water pollution.

Many mammals are threatened by illegal hunting. Where food is scarce in places such as central Africa, people often kill gorillas, buffalo, and other large mammals to feed their families. Throughout Africa and Southeast Asia, elephants are hunted for their ivory tusks, tigers for their bones, and rhinos for their horns.

Tropical and other forest habitats are quickly disappearing as trees are cleared to make room for farms, pastures, and other uses. When habitats are destroyed, local animals have nowhere to live. **Deforestation** also contributes to the warming of our planet, a process called global warming. This causes weather patterns to change and the polar ice caps to shrink.

CHAPTER 4

Reproduction and Communication

Different types of mammals give birth to their young in different ways. Humans, dogs, whales, bats, and many other familiar animals are placental mammals. Placental mammals give birth to live young. Before birth, the young grow inside the mother's body, getting oxygen and nourishment from a specialized tissue called the placenta. Once they are born, the young can live outside the mother's body, but still need care and feeding before they can survive on their own.

Grizzly bear cubs are usually born as twins.

Life Cycle: From Puppy to Dog

A male and female dog mate, then go their separate ways. Fertilized eggs, or embryos, begin to grow inside the mother's body.

Puppies are born when they have grown enough to survive outside the mother. They are born blind and deaf.

The puppies grow and learn survival skills from their mother until they are old enough to take care of themselves.

The mother nurses her litter with rich milk. She also cares for and protects them.

Pouches and Eggs

Most marsupials are found in Australia and New Guinea. Marsupials are born very underdeveloped. A newborn kangaroo is blind, hairless, and only about 1 inch (2.5 centimeters) long! After birth, the infant, or joey, climbs its mother's belly to her pouch, where the joey nurses on its mother's rich milk. The joey stays inside the pouch for several months, until it is large enough to move around on its own.

Australia and New Guinea are also home to monotremes, or egg-laying mammals. The platypus and the echidna are monotremes. The female platypus digs a burrow, lays her eggs, and keeps them warm until they hatch. When they do, the mother cares for her infants like any other mammal. Monotremes feed their young milk by secreting it from patches on their belly. The baby laps up milk from its mother's skin.

How Mammals Communicate

Humans use sound (language) to communicate with one another. So do many other mammals, including cats (growling and hissing), dogs (barking), and lions (roaring). Mammals also use body language to communicate. A hissing cat may arch its back or crouch in an attack position. A barking dog may bare its teeth if it feels threatened. A bark accompanied by a wagging tail usually means something else altogether—excitement!

An arched back means the cat is feeling threatened and afraid.

Lions can obtain information about another lion from the animal's scent marker.

On the Scent

When your dog stops to urinate on every tree, it is marking its territory by leaving its scent for other dogs. Otters leave piles of droppings, and lions spray jets of urine on trees and shrubs to mark their territory. Some mammals use scent to find a mate. Others rely on it to identify one another. Some scientists argue that humans give off a scent when they are afraid. This would warn other humans that there is potential danger.

One way humans have become a successful species is by caring for their young, making sure they grow up healthy and strong.

CHAPTER 5

The World's Most Successful Mammal

Members of a successful species survive long enough to leave behind plenty of offspring. This ensures the species will continue. The most successful species are able to survive in a variety of circumstances. They can eat a variety of foods, in case a food source disappears. They are also intelligent enough to learn and adapt to new situations. As a result, these species have large populations living in a range of habitats.

← There are about 7 billion humans on Earth.

Humans or Rats?

Humans and rats are both very successful mammals. Is one more successful? Large numbers of both live around the world. Humans can modify the environment to survive. They build shelter and produce food as needed. Rats eat almost anything and can solve problems to access food and shelter.

A rat also has lots of offspring, often 80 a year! But no matter what the most successful mammal is, all of the many mammals worldwide are essential to life on Earth.

Rats are creative. If a rat can't fit its mouth into a jar, it will use a paw.

Wolves in Yellowstone

When Yellowstone National Park was created in 1872, mammals living in the park, such as gray wolves, were not protected. People were free to hunt them. By 1926, there were almost no wolves left in Yellowstone. In the 1970s, the federal government made plans to reintroduce wolves into the park. The first were released in 1995. Since then, the wolf population has grown. Unfortunately, not everyone is happy. Farmers in surrounding areas fear that wolves will attack their livestock. On the other hand, more people are visiting the park to see wolves. ★

Length of the blue whale, largest animal on Earth: 100 ft. (30.5 m)

Weight of a blue whale's tongue: 8,000 lb. (3,628.7 kg)

Length of a giraffe's tongue: 20 in. (50.8 cm)

Number of giant pandas remaining in the wild: 1,000 to 2,000

Weight of the bumblebee bat, the smallest mammal on Earth: 0.07 oz. (2 grams)

Height of the world's tallest giraffe: 22 ft. (6.7 m), or as tall as four humans standing on top of one another

Largest number of puppies born in one litter: 24; the mother was Tia, a Neapolitan mastiff who gave birth to the litter of 9 females and 15 males in 2004

Did you find the truth?

F All mammals eat meat.

T All mammals produce milk for their young.

Resources

Books

Berger, Melvin, and Gilda Berger. *Mammals*. New York: Scholastic, 2011.

Caper, William. *The Platypus: A Century-Long Mystery*. New York: Bearport Publishing, 2009.

Racanelli, Marie. *Animals With Pockets*. New York: PowerKids Press, 2010.

Visit this Scholastic Web site for more information on mammals:
★ www.factsfornow.scholastic.com
Enter the keyword **Mammals**

Important Words

carnivores (KAHR-nuh-vorz) — animals that eat meat

class (KLAS) — a group of related plants or animals that is larger than an order but smaller than a phylum

deforestation (dee-for-iss-TAY-shuhn) — the removal or cutting down of forests

endothermic (ehn-doh-THURM-ik) — warm-blooded

extinct (ik-STINGKT) — no longer found alive

herbivores (HUR-buh-vorz) — animals that eat only plants

mammary glands (MA-muh-ree GLANDZ) — the large glands that in female mammals produce milk

placental (pluh-SEHN-tul) — having to do with the placenta, the tissue in most mammal mothers that nourishes a developing baby before it is born

primates (PRYE-mates) — members of the group of mammals that includes monkeys, apes, and humans

species (SPEE-sheez) — one of the groups into which animals and plants of the same genus are divided; animals of the same species can mate and have offspring

vertebrates (VUR-tuh-bruhts) — animals that have a backbone

Index

Page numbers in **bold** indicate illustrations

About the Author

Ann O. Squire is a psychologist and an animal behaviorist. Before becoming a writer, she studied the behavior of rats, tropical fish in the Caribbean, and electric fish from central Africa. Her favorite part of being a writer is the chance to learn as much as she can about all sorts of topics. In addition to writing *Reptiles*, *Mammals*, and *Birds* in the True Book series, Squire has written about many different animals, from lemmings to leopards and cicadas to cheetahs. She lives in Katonah, New York.